D E T O X
DECLUTTER
DOMINATE
HOW TO EXCEL BY ELIMINATION

PERRY MARSHALL
ROBERT SKROB

Publisher: Perry S. Marshall & Associates
805 Lake Street #295, Oak Park, IL 60301 USA
Phone: (312) 386-7459

ISBN: 978-1-7354211-0-0

www.PerryMarshall.com

About Your Authors

Perry Marshall

Perry Marshall is one of the most expensive business strategists in the world. Endorsed in Forbes and Inc. magazines, he has guided clients like LoanBuilder and InfusionSoft from start-up to hundreds of millions of dollars.

Perry founded the $10 million Evolution 2.0 Prize, with judges from Harvard, Oxford, and MIT. Launched at the Royal Society in London, it's the world's largest science research award.

NASA's Jet Propulsion Laboratory uses his 80/20 Curve as a productivity tool. His re-formulation of the Pareto Principle is published in Harvard Business Review.

Perry's Google book laid the foundations for the $100 billion Pay-Per-Click industry, and Ultimate Guide to Google Ads is the world's best-selling book on internet advertising.

Marketing maverick Dan Kennedy says, "If you don't know who Perry Marshall is—unforgivable. Perry's an honest man in a field rife with charlatans."

Robert Skrob

Robert Skrob worked with Perry Marshall and his team for more than three years to document and simplify Perry's New Renaissance business strategies into the book you are holding today. Taking the best 20%—8,000 words distilled from the original 40,000—made this a much stronger book.

Having spoken and conducted workshops on five continents, Robert is recognized as one of the best member retention specialists in the world. He works with subscription businesses including publishers, digital access, extended warranty, SAAS, coaching businesses, subscription boxes, and associations that range from start-up to $1.5 billion publishers.

In a world where obscene churn rates are all too common and even accepted, Robert is able to transform customer relationships he calls "one night stands" into long-term memberships.

Confessions of a Complexaholic

Four years ago on a snowy February day, I was talking on the phone. Suddenly the president of my company, Bryan, appeared in my office.

"Perry, we need to talk. Our expenses are too high. We need to cut. Cash flow is not good."

It was 2 p.m. We talked until late that night.

I spent all afternoon and the entire evening proving to Bryan he was wrong. I made a few concessions to him, but not many. My inner engineer-alchemist kicked into overdrive. "No, no, no, Bryan ... we're going to do this new promotion, and we're going to create this other thing, and this other project is about to pop in a really big way."

We kept on the same track for a couple more months.

And ... things got worse.

I was a respected business guru—but my business was facing problems. I was having trouble swallowing that. Bryan's visit was in February; in April, I was still fighting the notion that we needed to make major changes.

I finally realized: *we've got to lay people off.*

This was *sooo* disheartening. We'd been doing a fine job for some time. Our staff members had their tasks. The moving parts were flowing like a well-oiled machine.

But the machine was consuming too much money. Suddenly we had to figure out: how do we cut fat without cutting muscle and bone?

You can't cut business expenses with a hatchet. You have to cut with razor precision.

We held a "cutting" meeting every three days. Do we need this expense? Do we need this employee? Can we rearrange this job three people are doing so it only takes one? Every few days, the answers to these questions shifted as our perspective and assumptions changed. We continued to trim more and more.

Even my salary got slashed. Not fun.

After three or four months of painful subtracting, our ship started to right itself. We cut staff 40%; we slashed all kinds of expenses; my wife and I cut our personal expenses. Now our vessel was far easier to steer and took a lot less fuel to propel.

My ego was bruised. But everything else in my business and life was healthier. Our pace was slower and much more sane. My stress month to month plummeted.

When we subtracted everything that had a negative return on investment, we were able to redirect money into projects with positive ROI. This "multiply by subtracting" approach saved our business, and it can make any business better.

But there was another unexpected payoff:

As we began to solve problems by subtracting (instead of adding and multiplying) we began thinking in fresh terms. I started to see the power of subtracting other ways.

We helped our client Swift Capital radically subtract complexity from small business loans. They created LoanBuilder, which was acquired by PayPal. RoofSimple subtracted friction not only for roofing customers but also for contractors.

I told myself, *Perry, you need to create a path for people to subtract! People need to subtract expenses and email and social media. They need to purge phone addictions and toxic relationships ... they need to fire clients, subtract complexity from the customer experience, strip their lives and businesses down to the true 80/20 essentials ...*

Are You Willing to Go to Any Length?

In high school or college, did you have to read the epic poem *Beowulf*? I did. I'm guessing most were bored by it.

I didn't grasp its true meaning until I was in my late 40s.

King Hrothgar has built an impressive beer hall. All his merry men love to come together and drink there every night. But there's a problem: Grendel, an evil monster, shows up every now and then, kicks down the door, demolishes the place, and slaughters the knights and soldiers. The killings are resulting in a lot of bad Google reviews for Hrothgar.

Enter Beowulf. He's a hired gun. Not terribly different from a great many entrepreneurs—guys and gals who solve problems nobody else can solve.

A few nights later, Grendel kicks down the door and goes swashbuckling through the mead hall, smashing warriors and terrifying everyone.

Beowulf removes his iron breastplate to face Grendel with no armor or equipment whatsoever. Instead, Beowulf relies on his secret superpower: the mighty death grip of his own right hand.

Beowulf grasps Grendel by the shoulder and literally rips shoulder and arm right out of the socket and tosses them onto the floor. Grendel stomps back to the swamp from which he came and plunges into the water, leaving a trail of blood and gore.

BEOWULF

THE OLDEST ENGLISH EPIC
translated into alliterative verse with a critical introduction by
Charles W. Kennedy

Grendel is dead! A great toast is raised to Beowulf!

But the story is only one-third over.

A few nights later, *another* monster kicks down the door.

It's Grendel's mother. And she is MAD.

As poet and essayist David Whyte puts it in his excellent book *The Heart Aroused*, "It is not the thing you fear that you must deal with, it is the mother of the thing you fear."

How many entrepreneurs have solved a perceived difficulty at the first stroke only to realize it was merely a symptom of a deadlier disease at the heart of the business?

Back to the poem: Beowulf dives to the bottom of the swamp to confront the new monster. The swamp is so dreadful that even a deer being chased by wolves would rather get eaten than dive in. But Beowulf dives in anyway. He brings a magnificent sword given to him by Hrogarth ... and loses it almost immediately.

Grendel's mom attacks him in a rage and the only thing that keeps Beowulf alive is his chain mail. He manages to wriggle free, and just when she's about to impale him, he spies an ancient sword, seizes it, and takes a swing at Grendel's mother. The new sword slices all the way to the bone, killing her instantly.

What got you to the edge of the swamp will not serve you down in the swamp. The solution itself lies down in the depths.

I bet the Beowulf saga describes every big, ugly, badass problem you've ever solved in your life. It does for my life.

It's me getting a sales job and being thrown into the cold-calling swamp. I nearly lost my life, but then I discovered direct marketing.

It's me hanging out my shingle to become a marketing consultant, and then desperately needing sales leads. Writing articles and getting publicity put a patch on the problem for a while, but I didn't really solve it until I mastered Google Ads.

You have a monster to kill. The weapons others gave you don't work. You have to find new superpowers ... your own gleaming sword at the bottom of the swamp.

These 7 STEPS Aren't Only a List of Things to Do but a Shift in Worldview

No matter what you are doing now

WHEN YOU LEARN TO VIEW THE WORLD THROUGH THIS LENS

EVERYTHING CHANGES

Embracing these steps will open you up to limitless applications everywhere in your business and your life.

But remember, it won't be easy.

There will be dragons. And the worst dragons hide within those voices inside your own head.

The 7 Steps to Finding Your Gleaming Sword at the Bottom of the Swamp

The reason Beowulf was successful is that he was **willing to go where nobody else was willing to go.**

Are you ready to go where others do not dare?

If you are, I provide you these steps to the bottom of the swamp. These are the essential steps to creating a massive business, and a legacy that will last for generations. But remember, it won't be easy. There will be dragons. And the worst dragons hide within those voices inside your own head.

Here are the 7 Steps:

1. **Use Renaissance Time to Gain Discernment and Clarity**

2. **Make Your Business 2X More Profitable with 80/20 Focus**

3. **Earn $1,000/Hour at Least One Hour a Day With 80/20 Time**

4. **Create an Irresistible Product That's a Joy to Use—by Simplifying**

5. **Carve Out the Niche Where You're the Undisputed #1 Via the Star Principle**

6. **Build an Impenetrable Moat Around Your Business**

7. **Enjoy Freedom to Create and Reinvent Every Single Day**

Entrepreneurship is a riddle. The 7 Steps are the mindset that positions you to solve the riddle.

Here's a riddle to demonstrate what I mean:

You're pushing your car. You stop in front of a hotel. Suddenly you realize you're bankrupt.

Where are you?

[Answer on next page ... please stop reading now and see if you can figure this out.]

Answer:
You're on a Monopoly board.

With riddles, the answer is always obvious—*in hindsight.*

To solve all riddles, you have to ask questions and start eliminating options:

"Is the car a Chevy?" *No.*

"Can you drive this car the way you drive a Chevy?" *No.*

"Is the car a toy?" *Yes.*

"Is the hotel a hotel you can stay in like a Marriott?" *No.*

"Is the hotel one inch tall?" *Yes.*

You get the idea ... only by stabbing the problem with lots of questions do you arrive at the SPECIFIC conclusion: a toy car and a miniature hotel. You're bankrupt because you're on a Monopoly board.

All true success formulas are like this: a set of keys to unlock the questions using principles (i.e., guiding questions) to get at the answer/truth.

If you succeed at solving even ONE of the riddles of the 7 Steps, you'll make a decent living.

If you solve two or three, you'll be on your way to the financial success and liberties of your dreams.

I want to start a New Renaissance. The first Renaissance was 500 years ago. We're long overdue for another.

I'm dead serious. This is why I call my membership club "New Renaissance." And it's no coincidence that I'm doing this with ... *entrepreneurs*.

Entrepreneurs are THE class of people who can least afford to be wrong or misguided. Entrepreneurs have tremendous skin in the game, so we feel the pain acutely when we make mistakes. Entrepreneurs have to know a little bit about a *lot* of things and a great deal about quite a few things.

Entrepreneurs are curious and obsessive. Entrepreneurs are holistic because we know both problems and solutions can come from *anywhere*.

Many entrepreneurs are camouflaged because they don't own businesses. I know many scientists who have done groundbreaking work. I consider them entrepreneurs because while they may receive a salary from a large institution, they still defy norms, break rules, take risks, endure scorn and rejection for their views, and dare to craft a bold future. The very best entrepreneurs dive to the bottom of ugly swamps and solve problems most people were trying to pretend didn't exist.

If a mere ONE PERCENT of the people in the world commit to the 7 Steps, it will tip the world into an actual New Renaissance.

I realize my "one percent" number sounds outlandish. But 100 years from now, 1% of people will have shaped 99% of history. The Renaissance 1%.

I believe it is possible to solve hunger.

I believe it is possible for everyone in the world to be able to afford to stay healthy.

I believe it is possible for everyone in the world to receive a good education.

I am asking you to commit to the 7 Steps for the next two years—then look back and see how far they have carried you.

Yeah, I know. Two years seems like a long time, but you'll be a lot happier in two years if you commit to these 7 Steps now.

7 Steps to Business Renaissance

STEP 1
Use Renaissance Time to Gain Discernment and Clarity

At its heart, Renaissance Time is listening. Listening to whatever you call God, the Muse, or the Head Office. This is the most enjoyable and productive way to begin your day. When you commit to Renaissance Time, you'll find you actually have more time to think about important profit-building ideas.

STEP 2
80/20 2X

Make Your Business 2X More Profitable with 80/20 Focus

Increase your profits by 50% or more by discovering that 20% of your customers will spend four times the money to get something far better. Slash your expenses and hassle by subtracting clients and products that are invisibly losing money.

STEP 3
Earn $1,000/Hour at Least One Hour a Day With 80/20 Time

Most entrepreneurs do not set boundaries around their day. They let people interrupt them. They fail to delegate. Your mission is to spend as much time as you can on $100/hour, $1,000/hour, and $10,000/hour work. Then delegate, eliminate, or automate the rest.

STEP 4
Create an Irresistible Product That's a Joy to Use—by Simplifying

There are two ways to simplify, and they are radically different:
1. Make your product cheaper to make (subtract cost), or
2. Make your product a joy to use (subtract difficulty).

How to Grow Your Business 4X Faster by Eliminating 80% of Your Wasted Efforts

Here are the essential steps to creating a massive business, and a legacy that will last for generations.

STEP 5

Carve Out the Niche Where You're the Undisputed #1 Via the Star Principle

Almost all the money and growth comes from companies that are #1 in a market growing 10% or more per year. If you're not #1 in the growing market, carve off a slice of that market where there is no leader and become the leader.

STEP 6

Build an Impenetrable Moat Around Your Business

Scaling a business is impossible if your product or service is easy to replicate. Someone is always willing to do what you do, only cheaper. The first step to building a business that's immune to competitors is to become consciously aware of the protections you can put into place to take advantage of network effects.

STEP 7

Enjoy Freedom to Create and Reinvent Every Single Day

The biggest breakthroughs come by giving yourself time to think and staying connected to likeminded entrepreneurs. Do things that inspire you to feed your creativity engine.

Use Renaissance Time to Gain Discernment and Clarity

Renaissance Time is time you spend in meditation, prayer, journaling, reading ancient texts, yoga, or walking alone with your thoughts. NO phone calls. NO radio. NO TV. NO podcasts.

At its heart, Renaissance Time is *listening*. Listening to whatever you call the universe, God, or the muse. You must start every day this way.

How to Do Renaissance Time

Every morning I get out of bed, shower, boil some tea, and sit down with my notebook. Then, with no texting, no emails, no social media, no phone calls, no obligations, I write.

Write what?

Anything. As long as I'm writing ... and as long as my editor is switched OFF.

If you are engaging your brain and consciously trying to "push" what you are writing in a specific direction, you're doing it wrong. You must switch your editor off. Only then does your intuitive voice step up.

Renaissance Time doesn't *consume* your time. It *gives* you time.

People universally tell me that this morning discipline opens up their schedule rather than crowds it. *The busier you are, the more you need to do this.* Martin Luther accomplished as much during his life as anyone. He is the man who translated the Bible from Latin to the language for the masses and started the Protestant movement. He said, "I have so much to do that I shall spend the first three hours in prayer."

Read something written before Gutenberg every day.

Anything written before Gutenberg invented the printing press in the West, approximately 1450 AD, that we still have today survived the sacking of Rome and the burning of Alexandria. Only the REALLY good stuff made it through. Principles, not techniques. Timeless truths that will be just as true a thousand years from now as they were a thousand years ago.

Gutenberg's development of the printing press is considered one of the key events marking the transition from the Middle Ages to the Renaissance. The ideas that Gutenberg's presses distributed led to a complete rebirth of society. A transformation from dogma to experiments. Exactly the same transformation we all need to make today.

Pre-Gutenberg publications are the ultimate antidote to social media. If you decide to NOT do social media until after your workday is done—and if you read something written before Gutenberg *before* your workday begins—you will be 10 times more poised, centered, peaceful, and confident.

A New Definition of Work

There are many kinds of work, but we sloppily label all of them "work." My collaborator John Fancher and I created "The Four Quadrants of Work."

The Four Quadrants of Work

Barnacles is the lowest form of work. Driving packages to the post office when you should be straightening out a conflict. Scrolling mindlessly through Facebook. Hitting refresh on your email box every 2½ minutes. Jumping onto Twitter when you should be responding to an urgent email.

Sweetness is setting aside work entirely and enjoying an evening with your family. It's taking Sunday off and not checking emails. It's going on vacation.

Work Ethic is making $100 or $1,000 an hour doing what you're clearly good at for clients who write you a check.

Renaissance Time is still work—do *not* confuse it with Sweetness—but it's unpredictably productive. It's serendipitous and exploratory. At its best, it feels like play. Sometimes it's playing hard after you've worked hard.

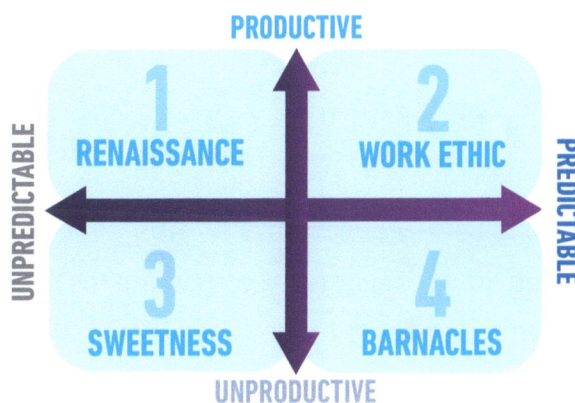

PRODUCTIVE

	1 RENAISSANCE	2 WORK ETHIC	
UNPREDICTABLE			PREDICTABLE
	3 SWEETNESS	4 BARNACLES	

UNPRODUCTIVE

The idea of starting your day with 20+ minutes of Renaissance Time and ignoring your devices is simple. But it's still hard. It has to be NONNEGOTIABLE.

I have not missed a day in seven years. Sometimes it gets done on a plane. But I'll get up at 4 a.m. if I have to.

When you commit to Renaissance Time, you'll find you actually have *more* time to think about important profit-building ideas, like espresso machines ... that's Step #2.

ACTION STEPS

1 Start your day without texting, social media, emails, or electronics.

2 Start your day analog: 20 minutes of free "spiritual space" with a notebook and pen.

3 Read something written before Gutenberg every day.

FOR FURTHER STUDY:
Enjoy Freedom to Create and Reinvent Every Single Day

Finding an extra hour every day through the elimination of life's noise is the key to the freedom to think and reinvent your life, your business, and your world. These secrets are ONLY taught in 30 Day Reboot and are practiced by hundreds of our members every day.

www.PerryMarshall.com/nextreboot

Make Your Business 2X More Profitable with 80/20 Focus

Inside every business is dozens, even hundreds of 80/20 levers, tiny hinges that swing big doors. 4% of what you do makes 64% of your profits. 10% of your products and clients lose more money than they make!

The 80/20 rule, aka the Pareto Principle, says:

1. 80% of what you get comes from 20% of what you do: Small Effort, Big Reward.
2. 20% of what you get comes from the other 80%: Big Effort, Small Reward.

80/20 applies to nearly anything you can measure in a business.

Sources of incoming phone calls, sizes of commissions for salespeople, spending by customers, physical location of customers, popularity of products, and sources of product defects can all benefit from applying the 80/20 principle.

This means four-fifths of everything is trivial and only one-fifth really matters. This is a huge time saver. But that's only the tip of the iceberg.

The 80/20 Principle Shows Up Everywhere
Here's an example of the 80/20 principle in action within the Fortune 500 represented by the blue line:

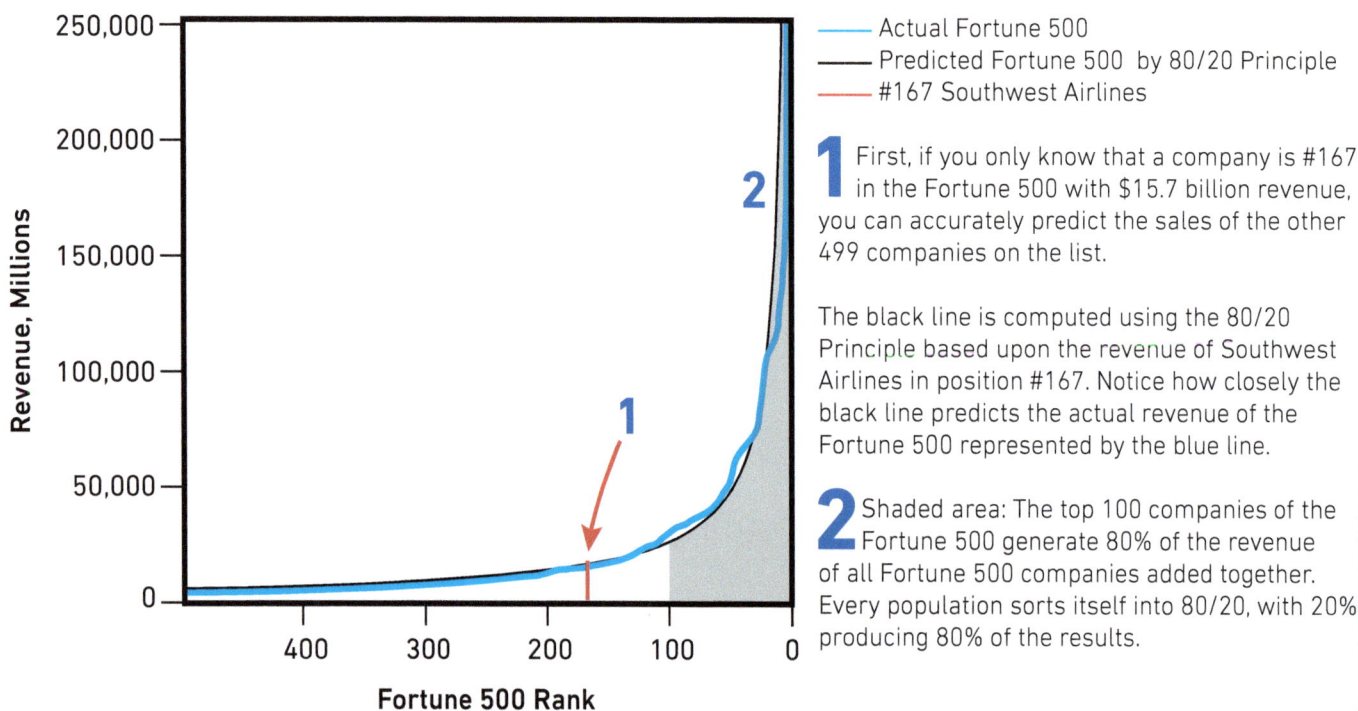

Legend:
— Actual Fortune 500
— Predicted Fortune 500 by 80/20 Principle
— #167 Southwest Airlines

Y-axis: Revenue, Millions (0 to 250,000)
X-axis: Fortune 500 Rank (400, 300, 200, 100, 0)

1 First, if you only know that a company is #167 in the Fortune 500 with $15.7 billion revenue, you can accurately predict the sales of the other 499 companies on the list.

The black line is computed using the 80/20 Principle based upon the revenue of Southwest Airlines in position #167. Notice how closely the black line predicts the actual revenue of the Fortune 500 represented by the blue line.

2 Shaded area: The top 100 companies of the Fortune 500 generate 80% of the revenue of all Fortune 500 companies added together. Every population sorts itself into 80/20, with 20% producing 80% of the results.

80/20 isn't just two groups, "the 80" and "the 20."

If you put 80/20 on a graph, it looks like the curve below.
This is *very* powerful for entrepreneurs. I created a tool called the 80/20 Curve (www.8020curve.com), and it reveals where you're missing opportunities.

There's an 80/20 inside every 80/20.

80/20 still applies to what remains after you peel away the bottom 80%. Not only does 80% of your money come from 20% of your customers, but 80% of the 80% comes from 20% of the top 20%.

That means 4% of your customers create 64% of your income. That's $80/20^2$. And it's still true of the top 4%: 0.8% of your customers deliver 52% of your income. That's $80/20^3$. It keeps going until you run out of people.

You can overlay multiple 80/20s on top of each other and get even faster leverage.

Not only do you get 50% of your business from 1% of your customers, you likely get 25% of your profits from one of your 250 products. You could easily make 10% more profit by pampering five big customers and fattening the margins on that one product. You can make a lot more profit by getting rid of 10% of your products that lose you money every time you sell them.

80/20 vs. 95/5 vs. 99/1

The reason there are dozens of car companies in the world, but only one eBay, two ridesharing companies (Uber and Lyft), and only one Amazon is because auto manufacturing is *high friction*, but internet is *frictionless.*

Frictionless means the feedback loops that reinforce 80/20 happen much faster. Winners win faster. Losers lose faster.

What this means is that while the internet appears to make everyone more equal ... it actually makes us unequal!

So ... the brick and mortar world is 80/20, but the internet is 95/5. On the internet, 5% of the companies get 95% of the business.

If you look at the influence of people over timespans of two generations and longer, it's even more extreme than that. It's 99/1.

1% of people shape 99% of history.

You want to be one of the 1% who shapes 99% of history. That means you need a core strategy you can use for your entire life.

My 7 Steps are that strategy.
The 1% Renaissance.

80/20 2X

If only 1% of the people in the world embrace these seven steps, we will enter a New Renaissance. So ... what tangible step can you take to enter the top 1%?

Let's start by applying the 80/20 Principal to your pricing. See how on the next page...

Make Your Top Customers Three Times More Profitable With an "Espresso Machine"

Here is an incredibly useful way to restate the 80/20 Principle: 20% of your customers will spend four times the money to get something far better.

If 100 customers spent $100, 20 will spend $400. Four customers will spend $1,600. *And you don't need to get more customers to score the extra sales.*

The Espresso Machine Calculator
(Available at www.PerryMarshall.com/extras)

If this is your current price:	And you've had this many buyers:	Then these are your total earnings:
$100	100	$10,000
Then you can offer something at this price:	**And get this many buyers:**	**And earn this much more:**
$400	20	$8,000
$1,600	4	$6,400
$6,400	1	$6,400
	This is what you're leaving on the table:	**$20,800**

I call this "the principle of the $2,700 espresso machine." 80/20 says for every 1,000 people who spend $5 on a latte, one will buy a gleaming stainless-steel espresso machine.

Notice I didn't say "for every 1,000 people who buy a $5 latte, one will buy a $500 latte." Nobody is going to buy a $500 latte. But plenty of people will gleefully scratch their coffee itch with something far more expensive.

The easiest way to figure out what you'd sell for 10 times the money is to ask: *"How can I sell results, not procedures?"*

The easiest solution is to add an espresso machine at 3X, 10X, 20X the base price. I have clients across 100 industries who have switched from unprofitable to profitable with espresso machines.

The Pricing Strategy That's Paramount to Your Success

Most business owners assume their customers are all equal.

Instead, here's a handy fact that's one of the most powerful rules in business:

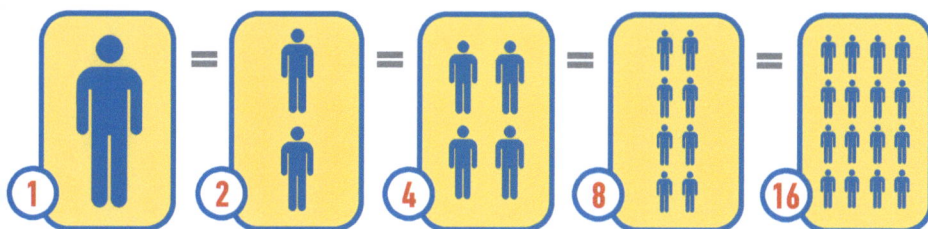

1 = 2 = 4 = 8 = 16

REAL WORLD EXAMPLE

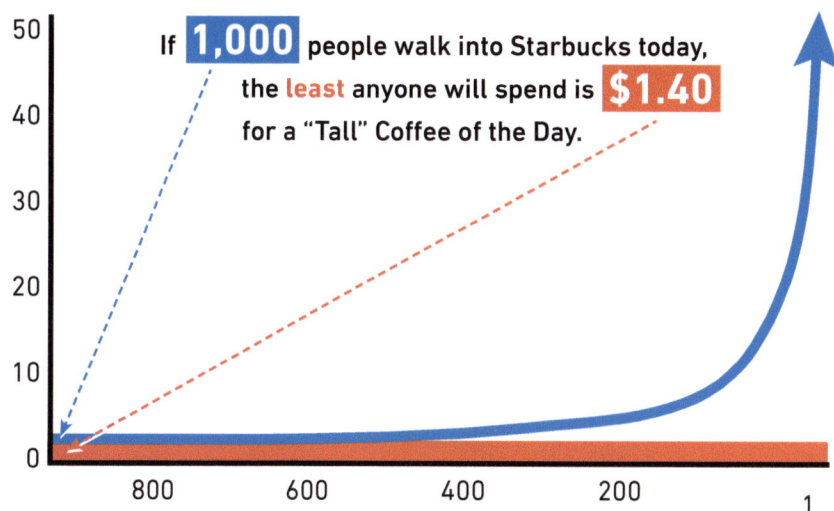

If **1,000** people walk into Starbucks today, the **least** anyone will spend is **$1.40** for a "Tall" Coffee of the Day.

We enter this data into the Power Curve calculator at **www.8020curve.com** and it reveals the **top customer** wants to spend **$537** at Starbucks today.

That's a lot of lattes!

Yes, but this is why Starbucks also sells espresso machines.

In fact, you can spend $275 for a machine from Starbucks or as much as $2,699.

When you have millions of customers every day around the world, a few individuals will be so passionate about coffee that they'll want to spend more.

THE 80/20 RULE

dictates that

20%

of the customers will spend

4X

the money of the average of your other 80 percent of your customers.

It also says

4%

of the people will spend

16X

your average customer value.

WHAT DOES THIS MEAN FOR YOU?

If you are focused on figuring out how to price your products and services as cheaply as possible

YOU ARE MISSING OUT ON MOST OF YOUR PROFITS.

Some of your customers will be willing to spend a lot more with you if you offer them the right product.

The EASIEST Way to Increase Your Business Profits

ADD AN "ESPRESSO MACHINE"
type product into your product offering at

3X, 10X, 20X
THE BASE PRICE

80/20 DICTATES THAT 50%
of your revenue wants to come from

1% OF YOUR CUSTOMERS

The easiest way to figure out what you'd sell for 10 times the money is to ask:

"HOW CAN I SELL RESULTS NOT PROCEDURES?"

success

The easiest solution is to add an espresso machine at 3X, 10X, 20X the base price. I have clients across 100 industries who have switched from unprofitable to profitable with espresso machines. Subject matter experts sell an introductory course or a masterclass for under $100. They add a $1,000 to $5,000 espresso machine, taking the form of personal calls, email access, and face-to-face training.

"Sell results, not procedures" is HARD WORK.
But you can't imagine how it will transform your industry once you pull it off.

Subject matter experts sell an introductory course or masterclass for under $100. They add a $1,000 to $5,000 espresso machine, taking the form of personal calls, email access, and face-to-face training.

Then, a second espresso machine: The expert will parachute into your business or life and completely manage your problem from start to finish—tens of thousands of dollars and more.

Providing personal services has a high profit margin and allows your business to be viable even at low sales volumes and with small numbers of customers. 80/20 dictates that 50% of your revenue *wants* to come from 1% of your customers. The espresso machine principle enables you to make this happen easily.

If you're mumbling, "I don't have anything to offer that is worth three times what I'm currently selling," then you need to find one, create one, partner or borrow one. If you sell "do it yourself," can you sell a "done for you" version that's 10 times as expensive?

Or can you sell a version of your service that is 10 times faster? Can you subtract complexity for the customer?

When you do this, you will get what we call an "emergent property." The emergent property is the new phenomenon you cannot predict when you move from one scale to another.

For example, Henry Ford "invented" the fast food industry, indirectly. *It emerged from his simplification of automobile assembly.* Cars necessitated drive-thru windows.

If you greatly simplify your customer's life, *something* will happen that you've never imagined. It may be obvious **after it happens**. For example, it would have taken a fair amount of imagination before Uber to realize that you could take an entire vacation and use a rideshare service to go *everywhere*.

"Sell results, not procedures" is HARD WORK. But you can't imagine how it will transform your industry once you pull it off. Then you'll be ready for Step #3: Earn $1,000/Hour at Least One Hour a Day.

ACTION STEPS

1 Use the Espresso Machine Calculator at www.PerryMarshall.com/extras to price your premium offer.

2 Offer a convenience or shortcut that nobody else provides.

3 Definition of convenience or shortcut: "Sell results, not procedures."

FOR FURTHER STUDY:
Make Your Top Customers Three Times More Profitable With an "Espresso Machine"

Increasing your customer's lifetime value is the key to building a profitable, sellable business and is easily accomplished through this extraordinary concept called the Espresso Machine Principle.

www.PerryMarshall.com/extras

Earn $1,000/Hour at Least One Hour a Day With 80/20 Time

Most people make $1,000 or more per hour for a few minutes here and there, multiple times a day. That money is earned during a few make-or-break moments during the week, but people are mostly unaware of this. This is true in all businesses of all sizes.

Income in your business has very little to do with what you are doing most hours of the day, and has everything to do with how you handle *mission critical minutes and seconds*.

Most highly paid executives waste large spans of time on low-value activities. Here are just a few of them. Rank your opportunities in dollars per hour:

$10 per hour	$100 per hour	$1,000 per hour	$10,000 per hour
Driving & errands	Problem solving for existing or prospective customers	Prioritizing your day	Honing your Unique Selling Proposition
Organizing & cleaning	Outsourcing basic tasks	Delegating sophisticated tasks	Creating superior offers
Cold calling; speaking with unqualified prospects	Talking to qualified prospects	Writing good copy	Repositioning your message & position

The typical $100,000-per-year person spends the great majority of time on trivial $10-per-hour tasks; a fair amount of time doing $100-per-hour jobs; and only occasionally—and somewhat accidentally—executing highly productive $1,000-per-hour tasks.

"But I'll never make $1,000 an hour for a whole hour."

You may be right ... at first. But you CAN make $1,000 an hour for a minute or two. By mending fences with an upset customer or intercepting a phone call before it goes to voice mail. That's a $150 to $300 gain.

As soon as you become conscious of this, you will find ways to expand it. Next thing you know, you save $800 with a five-minute phone call. That's $9,600 an hour for 1/12 of an hour. Then you start subtracting busywork and being more strategic ... a few weeks later you really do make $1,000 in one hour. Then you start doing it more.

Your mission is to spend as much time as you can on $1,000/hour and $10,000/hour work. Then delegate, eliminate, or automate the rest. $10,000 an hour work happens almost automatically once you've reached the absolute bottom of the swamp.

Is This Worth MY Time?

Questions for Your Staff to Answer BEFORE They Ask You a Question:

1. Will this influence a single purchase of $10,000 or more?

2. Will this improve our systems, impact more than $10,000 of sales, or affect our reputation?

3. Is it vital to ask me this because I am the only person who knows the answer?

4. Has the question already been directed to all other staff members and gone unanswered?

5. Is this feedback vital because it could shape the direction of the company?

6. Is the person involved a VIP (potential client, important colleague, influencer, industry leader)?

7. Does this involve significant spending of money?

8. Is it a significant media opportunity?

9. Does this affect my personal schedule, travel, family, or relationships?

10. Does this affect a project I am currently focused on?

Most entrepreneurs do not set boundaries around their day. They let people interrupt them. They fail to delegate.

Stop now. Lay down hard boundaries and delegate the tasks you don't need (or want) to do.

ACTION STEPS

1 Take a close look at this past week and ask: "When did my $1,000/hour and $10,000/hour moments occur?"

2 Get a personal assistant. (Watch our webinar on how to hire an ideal virtual assistant at www.PerryMarshall.com/extras.)

3 Move $10-per-hour tasks off your plate, for good.

4 Before you move on to Step #4, read my Lightning 80/20 Crash Course ... it's next.

FOR FURTHER STUDY:

Earn $1,000/Hour at Least One Hour a Day With 80/20 Time

Casting off your day-to-day drudgery is the key to opening up your time to truly productive work. We teach you to cut away the mindless work and do what is truly productive in 80/20 Productivity Express.

https://www.PerryMarshall.com/productivity

How to MULTIPLY Your Income by 1,000% or More

$10,000 PER HOUR

$1,000 PER HOUR

$100 PER HOUR

"CAN I GET A RAISE?"

Yes! How about a **raise** of a **thousand bucks** an **hour**?

You can increase your income by setting aside time each day to focus on $10,000-per-hour tasks and delegating or ignoring the $10-per-hour tasks.

When you move from doing $10-per-hour work to $10,000-per-hour work, the least valuable minute in your day is worth 19 cents and the most valuable minute in your day is worth $166 to you. Your growth creates opportunities for yourself as well as the people below you.

$10 PER HOUR

The point of making $100 or $1,000 or $10,000 per hour is **not to become a slave to your work but to be the master of it.** It's not about selling more; it's about getting your life back! It's about regaining a sense of control, of setting your own priorities. **It's about being able to take that three-week vacation and shut off your cell phone—without guilt.**

$10 per hour	$100 per hour	$1,000 per hour	$10,000 per hour
Running errands	Solving a problem for a prospective or existing customer	Planning & prioritizing your day	Improving your USP
Talking to unqualified prospects	Talking to a qualified prospect	Negotiating with a qualified prospect	Creating new & better offers
Cold-calling or emailing (of any variety)	Writing an email to prospects or customers	Building your sales funnel	Repositioning your message & position
Building & fixing stuff on your website	Creating marketing tests and experiments	Judging marketing tests & experiments	Getting to the bottom of the swamp
Doing expense reports	Managing Pay-Per-Click campaigns	Creating Pay-Per-Click campaigns	Subtracting customer complexity
Working "social media" the way most people do it	Doing social media well (this is rare)	Doing social media with extreme competence (this is very rare)	Selling to high-value customers & groups
Cleaning, sorting	Outsourcing simple tasks	Delegating complex tasks	Selecting team members
Spelling everything perfectly	Customer follow-up	Writing sales copy	Public speaking

3 SIMPLE STEPS TO GET MORE $10,000/HOUR WORK DONE

1 DIVIDE
Divide everything you do into $10-, $100-, and $1,000-per-hour tasks.

2 DELEGATE
Delegate or decline the $10-per-hour tasks to others, now. Eventually delegate the $100-per-hour tasks, too.

3 TRANSFORM
Fill some of the extra time with family and fun to increase your energy. Schedule the rest with $10,000 work that will transform your life.

Create an Irresistible Product That's a Joy to Use— by Simplifying

All businesses make something simpler for the customer.

The first guy to sell a gallon of milk simplified because his neighbor didn't have to raise a cow. The first guy to pave a road simplified by making chariots go faster.

There are two ways to simplify, and they are radically different:

1. Make your product cheaper to make (subtract cost).
2. Make your product a joy to use (subtract difficulty). iPad subtracts user complexity; Tesla subtracts "driving the car" from your to-do list; Amazon 1-click subtracts steps from the order process.

You do one or the other.

Not both!

The ditch most entrepreneurs fall into is: they try to do **two kinds of simplification at the same time**. They try to price simplify (a little) and proposition simplify (a little) at the same time. That never works. It's a recipe for failure.

The ideal price simplifier delivers 80% of the value for 20% of the price. A product or service where, due to some great innovation in producing it, the cost of delivery has been slashed. The value has been reduced, but the price advantage far exceeds what you've given up.

Example: No-frills Southwest Airlines. Soft drinks and pretzels; no meals; only 737s and coach seating. But it's easy, fast, and cheap.

The ideal proposition simplifier is 500% of the value for 120% of the price. A product or service where, due to some innovation, the speed or performance or enjoyment has been spiked.

Example: Tesla.

A little *better* and a little *cheaper* is a grand recipe for mediocrity.

"I'm going to make this a little better *and* a little cheaper." You end up with a product or service that does not *begin* to stand out.

One of the biggest mistakes I see beginners make is that they are trained to be *adequate*. Adequate doesn't cut it.

It's possible to do okay and make an okay living with an okay product. *But every industry on earth is a sitting duck for somebody bold to come along and simplify.* When they do, they will drive you right out of business in months. Maybe weeks.

Do you want to be the okay bed and breakfast owner who got his butt handed to him by Airbnb?

Maybe you won't come up with a breakthrough idea as killer as Airbnb. But you should never stop asking these questions. Never stop improving. Most businesses I look at could be improved 20% just by incremental improvements. Subtract 20% of the garbage. Tighten your critical processes by 20%.

If you're reading this, you're probably going to be a proposition simplifier. Proposition simplifier means "joy to use."

Watch a free video about how to proposition simplify at www.PerryMarshall.com/extras.

What shortcut can I provide to my customer that my competitors assume is impossible to deliver? What paved highway is my competition too lazy to build?

Next up is how to find your niche—in the meantime, don't forget to simplify!

ACTION STEPS

1 Ask yourself: "What will make my product 5X easier to use or 5X more useful?"

2 Ask yourself: "What will make my product easily worth the money even if it's the most expensive in its category?"

3 Do not stop asking these questions until you get an answer.

FOR FURTHER STUDY:
Create an Irresistible Product That's a Joy to Use—by Simplifying

To give you a greater understanding of the power of simplifying, I've included an in-depth audio/video interview with Richard Koch, author of *Simplify: How the Best Businesses in the World Succeed*, in the member's area. Grab it at

www.PerryMarshall.com/extras

Carve Out the Niche Where You're the Undisputed #1 Via the Star Principle

Star Principle by Richard Koch is required reading for all my clients.

Star Principle says:

- **Almost all the money and growth comes from companies that are #1 in a market growing 10% or more per year.**
- **If you're not #1 in the growing market, carve off a slice of that market where there is no leader and become the leader.**

As simple as these two points are, they create an almost endless rabbit hole because the Star Principle is so powerful. (I've included an in-depth audio/video interview with Richard Koch about Star Principle in the member's area. Grab it at www.PerryMarshall.com/extras.)

At its core, constructing a Star business is a Unique Selling Proposition (USP) salvo. USP is your answer to the question: "What guarantee can you make better than anybody and everybody else?"

I'm amazed at how many products, marketers, consultants, and entrepreneurs do not have a USP. Even people who by all rights *should* know better.

Whatever you sell, there is some unscratched itch. There is a further step that somebody wants you to take with your product or service. A basic "80/20 Survey" will accomplish this. You can find out how to create one at www.PerryMarshall.com/extras.

Is Your Business a 'Star Principle' Business?

What adjustments can you make to make it a Star? Is your new idea a Star? Find out in 60 seconds at https://www.PerryMarshall.com/star-principle

If you're always poking your head down rabbit holes, eventually one of them will open up into an underground system of caverns. A great opportunity bigger than you ever imagined.

Objection: "My industry isn't growing. It's completely commoditizing. It doesn't meet any of the requirements necessary for me to become a Star."

Well, first of all that's a recipe for not making any money. You're just duking it out with everybody over price and delivery, which is a race to the bottom. You have to ask the question, "What boiling frustration is just below the surface that nobody else is addressing?"

I am summoning entrepreneurs everywhere to do this. If you're selling *yet another whatever it is you sell,* you're in trouble. You have a bullseye on your head, and somebody is going to shoot you dead. If there is truly no way to simplify, no way to innovate, then get out of that business and do something else.

Objection: "There's already a #1 900-pound gorilla in my industry, and it's not me."

What are they **not** doing? There's always something they're not doing. There's always an unmet need. Do an 80/20 Survey (details at www.PerryMarshall.com/extras) and find out.

It all comes down to your USP. This is of prime importance because most people have never experienced what it's like to sell something so unique that people actually want it.

Life is *so much easier* when you're #1 in a growing market. When you're a Star. It's 100% worth the effort to get there.

Next I'll tell you how to build a moat around your success. Till then …

ACTION STEPS

1 Identify which part of your market is growing, and which is shrinking.

2 Identify the part of this growing market where none of your competitors are meeting a need.

3 Create a solution for this unserved niche.

FOR FURTHER STUDY:
Carve Out the Niche Where You're the Undisputed #1 Via the Star Principle

Positioning yourself correctly in the market and in the eyes of your customers is the key to shooting your business into the stratosphere. How to do this can only be found by tapping into the innovative knowledge of two of the world's leading experts in business strategy, Perry Marshall and Richard Koch.

www.PerryMarshall.com/meetrichard

Build an Impenetrable Moat Around Your Business

I t's easy to start a business. Creating an asset that *lasts a long time* is hard. Making it immune from competition is the most essential part of making it last. You need a 21st century moat around your castle.

21st century moats take advantage of the Network Effect. For example, Airbnb has the property listings *and* they also have the travelers. The travelers attract properties and properties attract travelers in a beautiful, virtuous circle.

It's easy to replicate Airbnb's website ... but nearly impossible to replicate their network. They could give away the source code for their website and still be immune from competition.

The purpose of this chapter is to raise your awareness of Network Effect so you can harness it, even on a much smaller scale.

Silicon Valley "unicorns" like PayPal, Airbnb, Uber, eBay, Facebook, and Zoom are all obviously driven by Network Effect as all are hubs that bring masses of people together. Each one required massive amounts of venture capital.

But small companies can still use less obvious but nonetheless effective forms of Network Effect that do not require large amounts of capital at all. I call this **"Network Effect for Mere Mortals."**

The first key to building invisible moats is to become aware of them yourself. Network Effect for Mere Mortals is often invisible to the casual observer but more powerful than traditional barriers to competition like manufacturing facilities, geography, and start-up capital. Network Effect For Mere Mortals is the gleaming sword at the bottom of the swamp:

Reviews: Once you gain momentum with reviews, it grows exponentially harder for your competition to catch up – because reviews attract more reviews. Often reviews can travel with you to new cities and countries, making expansion easier with time.

Speed: The magnetism of 2X speed is not 2X. It's more like 4X! Speed attracts speed. *Over time it will eventually attract four times as many customers.* The delay is transaction friction.

Feedback Loops: Reviews attract reviews. Expertise attracts expertise. Experience attracts experience. Data attracts data. Speed attracts speed. Purchasing power gets discounts, which increase volume and profits.

Online Communities: The value of a network is proportional to the number of members squared, so the more members you have in your network, the more powerful it is. Community attracts community.

Software As Service: Salesforce and InfusionSoft being two examples. The better the software, the more users it attracts. More users bring money to improve the software. Eventually, entire ecosystems spring up to support these SAS companies.

Service As Software: "Magic" is a service where you send a text message to a virtual support desk and they do just about anything you want. I had a friend who needed a cord of firewood delivered to his front door. He texted Magic, and two hours later, a guy showed up with firewood. Magic billed him for the firewood plus the time.

This is called "Service As Software" because you access it through your smart phone. So from the customer's point of view, it appears to be push-button simple. Behind the scenes it's manual labor and carefully crafted procedures. All the machinery of figuring out where to find firewood at 6:30 p.m. on a Saturday night in Amherst, Massachusetts – and how to get it delivered – is hidden from the customer. A competitor must be ridiculously committed in order to knock you off.

First Mover Advantage: If you're already in the market, you have the first mover advantage. Others may move into the same neighborhood, but you have the upper hand.

Membership Retention Strategies: The duration of average membership is THE #1 lever in a member or subscription business.

Proprietary Language: People in close communities have shared language that exists nowhere else... and this creates more shared language. In Planet Perry when you say, "I'm 80/20ing my task list today," people know exactly what you mean. Here, 80/20 is a verb.

Trust: If you are the most trusted person in your space, everything you say in our low-trust world is more believable. Trust attracts trustworthy people who create more trust. The foundation of all economic systems is trust.

Being Prolific: Every time you write another book, every other book you've written benefits. Every time you add a new video to your YouTube channel, you attract more viewers for the rest of your videos.

Data: If your competitor has 100 customers and you have 1,000, you can perform many tasks better than they can, simply because you have more data.

Simple Outside, Complex Inside: Crafting precise internal processes that are difficult to replicate.

Compound Friction Reduction: Early on, Google realized speed was more valuable than anything. That's why Google's home page is white; it loads faster. Their unswerving commitment to friction reduction accelerated everything else they did.

Combinations of ALL the above: Speed of reviews. Speed of feedback loops. Data on membership retention. Harnessing online communities to be more prolific.

Beware of Anti-Network Effect. Boredom can distract us from our heavily moated business into unknown regions. If you do say yes to outside things, make sure you're not cannibalizing your existing business. Most things you add to your business divert energy away from these self-reinforcing cycles.

ACTION STEPS

Identify where you are vulnerable.

Ask yourself: "What Network Effect elements are available to me that I've ignored?" There's always a few.

Ask yourself: "What friction can I reduce that will amplify and give me an expanding advantage?"

For Further Study:
Build an Impenetrable Moat Around Your Business

Standing out from the crowds shouting for your prospect's attention is the only way to ensure your business's stability in a competitive market. This can only be done by outlining your advantages and strengths through our innovative course, Definitive Selling Proposition.

www.PerryMarshall.com/dsp

Can Your Marketing and Selling Become Easier, Less Tedious, Less Frustrating, and More Rewarding?

Take this short, PERSONALIZED test and I'll deliver a 1 in 10,000 Customized Training Course & Profile Report based on YOUR Unique Marketing DNA.

Many sales and marketing courses SAY "everyone can do it" and "this works for everyone" and "this is a system and the system never fails."

The truth is, if something's worth paying money for, NOT anyone can do it, nor should they. There are some sales and marketing tasks that you excel at and others that drive you crazy.

Even if you are brand new, a combination of selling skills you already have place you in the top 10%. You just need to know what your key skills are and what arena you should compete in.

The Marketing DNA Test answers this and shows what to pursue and what to avoid. It also helps you assign tasks to employees and find freelancers and team members who bring exactly what you lack.

Take the Marketing DNA Test at www.MarketingDNATest.com.

Enjoy Freedom to Create and Reinvent Every Single Day

There are two kinds of Renaissance Time:

1. **Reflection.** Spiritual space (first thing in the morning) so you can listen. This is your foundation.
2. **Exploration.** The upper left quadrant—unpredictable, occasionally productive, "non-work-ethic" engagement.

Renaissance exploration is *unpredictably productive.* Step #7 is complementary to grounding yourself, through your habit of beginning your day free of digital noise and doing meditation, prayer, watching ducks in a pond, yoga, or pre-Gutenberg reading. But it's not the same.

As you clear out your barnacles, your "work ethic" time accomplishes more with less effort. This frees you for positive exploration, which becomes a whole new dimension of work. Because it's not really work ... it's play!

This is the most pleasurable form of subtracting.

I have strong workaholic tendencies. I always need to be doing something. Today, 20% to 40% of my day is unpredictably productive Renaissance Time (exploration, not morning ritual reflection). If you're a fly on the wall, I still look like I'm "working," but most of that is exploratory projects.

I don't read many business books; 99% are boring and predictable. My best business ideas come from outside of business. I attend conferences that have nothing to do with business. I explore questions that have nothing to do with marketing. I write books that have nothing to do with my main profession.

Step #7 feeds your creativity engine, your inner artist. It's *doing things that inspire you.* Pursuing ideas that mostly may not work out. It's meeting a friend of a colleague far outside your normal circle, where there's a 95% chance it's merely an interesting lunch date, but a 5% chance it turns into something remarkable and unexpected.

There are three reasons why I can spend one or two hours in reflective Renaissance Time every day, ride my bike 100 miles a week, take international trips, and build stereo equipment when I feel like it ...

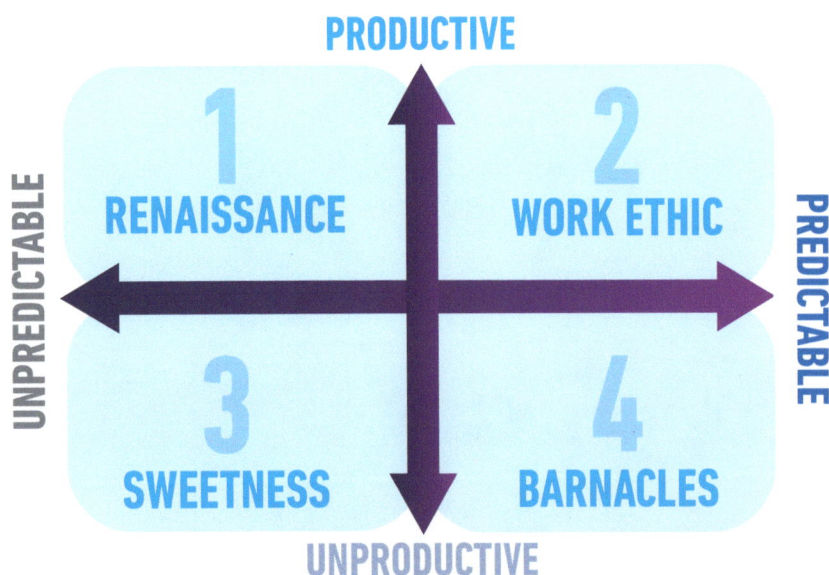

PRODUCTIVE

UNPREDICTABLE

1 RENAISSANCE	2 WORK ETHIC
3 SWEETNESS	4 BARNACLES

PREDICTABLE

UNPRODUCTIVE

while also having four kids, adopting two more, founding a science prize, running five companies, and authoring a half dozen books.

It's not because I've got "screw you" money. I still work for a living. The reasons are:

1) My wife is awesome.
2) I'm ruthless about Step #1, Renaissance Time, because reflection and exploration don't take time. They make time.
3) I'm ruthless about Step #3, make $1,000/hour one hour a day.

You need space to think. To breathe. To cultivate relationships. Maybe it's taking a weekend off and going somewhere with your spouse.

You are not your business!

If somehow you have absorbed the idea that you do not have the right to enjoy anything or feel a sense of satisfaction "until (fill in the blank)" ...

... that day may never come.

If you're taking risks most people don't have the courage to take, then that's worthy of respect ALL BY ITSELF.

Stop punishing yourself and take some time to smell the roses. And be sure to stay connected with likeminded entrepreneurs. Next, we'll tackle solutions to the isolation and loneliness that can arise when you work exclusively online.

ACTION STEPS

1 If you struggle with guilt about doing things you love, subscribe to the email series at www.PerryMarshall.com/headtrash.

2 Figure out what drains your energy and delete or delegate it.

3 Figure out what energizes you and do more of it.

FOR FURTHER STUDY:

Enjoy Freedom to Create and Reinvent Every Single Day

Finding an extra hour every day through the elimination of life's noise is the key to the freedom to think and reinvent your life, your business, and your world. These secrets are ONLY taught in 30 Day Reboot and are practiced by hundreds of our members every day.

www.PerryMarshall.com/notify

From In-Laws' Basement to Explosive Star Business: The Mark McShurley Story

Mark McShurley is a 32-year-old CEO. Three and a half years ago, he was chewing anxiety pills and living in a relative's basement with his wife and four kids. Today he's sneaking up on his industry and catching them by surprise. Here's Mark's story of multiplying by subtracting.

I began this booklet with my story of subtracting from a well-established but bloated business. I conclude this booklet with the story of a desperate guy in a pure start-up who subtracted from ... almost nothing.

After reading Perry Marshall and Richard Koch, I was 80/20ing everything I could. Soon I had built a pretty comfy gig for myself as the general manager of a roofing company. I had streamlined the systems and only had to work about 25 hours a week. Cushy.

Then the market sagged. I had to go out and drum up business myself. I hated it.

My cozy little life became very uncomfortable, and I realized it was time to do my own thing.

My friend Marty ran a construction business. He was itching to get out of the "reinvent the wheel every day" thing, too. So, I left the other roofing company, and we started Roof Simple.

In our first full year, we did 30 roofs. Barely enough money to keep us alive. I had my first panic attack around this time.

Three weeks later we moved into my in-laws' basement in Minnesota.

We were broke. Worse than broke: In debt. Negative money.

We didn't shut down Roof Simple. We just stopped paying *me* while I licked my wounds. That saved the company a lot of money.

While the roofing business trudged along, I got a job selling bulletin advertising. That's when the panic attacks got worse.

My therapist said, "With anxiety, if you keep running it's only gonna get worse. You have to lean in and face it and start getting stronger."

I took a course with Perry that combined a 30 Day Reboot with digital advertising.

Perry gave me a piece of basic business advice that almost nobody takes: build profit margin into your business. I added margin into the calculators we used to price jobs. I eliminated some expenses. I let go of an employee who was not carrying his weight.

When you're broke, the temptation is to lower your standards. You're thinking, "I just need money today." But raising my standards was what made this whole thing start working. Holding fast to the Star Principle made it take off. I can't overstate the importance of principles.

I subtracted ... my job.

I was traveling around selling bulletin advertising, making 100 to 150 calls a day to local businesses. I had no Renaissance Time. So, I quit my ad sales job.

Roof Simple income was still barely enough to keep us alive, but quitting gave me way more time.

And it revitalized me. I felt the fire again.

Renaissance Time gave me the perspective and guts to make a few big changes in our operations and customer experience.

Other roofers were tolerating irritations, complications and friction points that made the customer experience unpleasant. We started hiring an entirely different breed of salesperson who is not infected with the diseases of the roofing industry. Our agreements with subcontractors also have better terms and fewer friction points.

We lavished attention on customers by putting a concierge on site. We focused on getting 5 star reviews to an extreme degree. Simplifying made us a Star business by default, because no one else in the market was doing these things. Roof Simple not only has 500+ online reviews, we also have faster "review velocity" than anyone else in the roofing business. A strong moat.

This is how we grew an unsexy business from under $1 million to over $10 million, in an overall market that's hardly growing.

Three years later, Perry brags about how we are poised to take over the roof industry ... and he's right. We are quietly engineering a revolution.

You need to break the activity addiction. There is no inherent virtue in activity. The only way you'll ever get off the hamster wheel is ... *get off the hamster wheel.*

Beginning of the New Renaissance

If you're an online entrepreneur, or really any kind of entrepreneur, most of your friends and family don't understand what you do. (And they never will.)

First of all, most people work "regular jobs." And they don't speak the entrepreneurial tongue.

Second, even the ones that do understand are not in the same industry you're in, they don't use the same tools you use, and they're not at your ambition level. You can't go to the church potluck and complain about your $400,000 tax bill.

Third, many entrepreneurs are natural lone wolves. We default to "do it myself, by myself," and we need to intentionally shift ourselves out of our default setting. We need to get out and around the people who *get* us.

I don't think entrepreneurs appreciate how powerful and efficient we are when we immerse ourselves in a group where everybody around you understands 80/20.

It does you *so much good* to 1) leave your cave; 2) be with people who get you and validate your struggle; 3) be with people who speak your language; 4) confront questions you never would have thought to ask yourself; and 5) soak up the life-giving energy of people who are striving to make their world a better place.

I can't really explain it, but something magical happens when people get together. Maybe it's metaphysical. Or maybe it's just super-physical. Whatever it is, it extends beyond whatever knowledge, facts, approaches, or techniques you get from some webinar or reading a book.

When I am physically present with the sharpest people I can find, it's like shaving with brand new razor blades. I slice through problems faster and easier.

If you're committed to your business, decide:

"I'm going to go to everything that's appropriate for me."

That's the approach I take with my own education. For about 25 years, my wife and I have asked, "Will it help us?" "Can we afford it?" is always a distant second.

In *Outliers*, Malcolm Gladwell documents that, in Canada, if a student is one of the oldest in his class, he has a much higher chance of being a professional hockey player someday than the younger students in the same class. A slight difference (a few months) amplified, amplified, and amplified mushrooms into a huge benefit over time.

Same with you, dear entrepreneur. If you consistently insert yourself into communities where the expectation is high, that difference will amplify. And amplify and amplify.

If you stay in your cave? You miss the amplification factor, and you may even devolve and get smaller.

When I introduced the 7 Steps, I said I believe it is possible to solve hunger; for everyone to get a good education; for us to solve the BIG problems in the world. These things will only happen when we bring fresh entrepreneurial thinking to the world's most pressing problems.

So, let's start a New Renaissance together. The New Renaissance begins today ... with you.

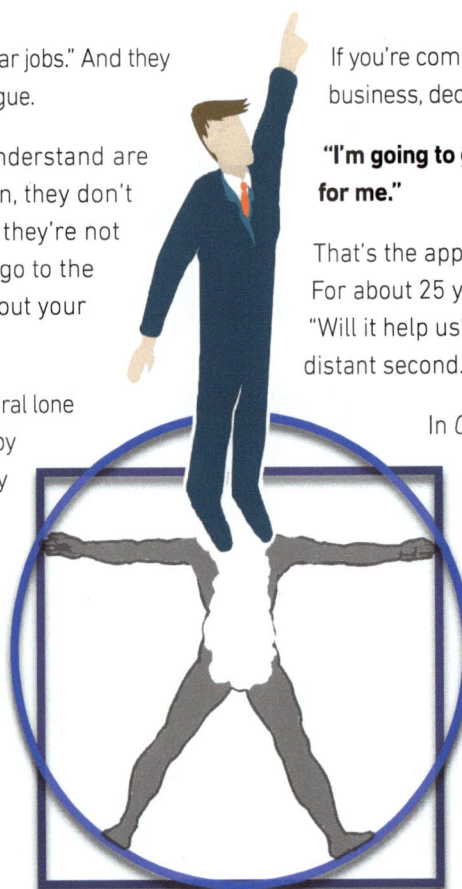

www.ingramcontent.com/pod-product-compliance
Lightning Source LLC
Chambersburg PA
CBHW052046190326
41520CB00003BA/206